Dear
ASSHOLE

101 TEAR-OUT LETTERS TO THE
MORONS WHO MUCK UP YOUR LIFE

Jillian Madison &
Michelle Madison

RUNNING PRESS
PHILADELPHIA

LEGAL DISCLAIMER

Use of company and product names is not authorized by, associated with, or sponsored by any trademark owner, and is intended for literary effect only. Dear Asshole is a humor book. Its advice and suggestions are meant to make you laugh and are not intended to be taken seriously. Please use common sense and don't be a moron. The authors and publisher disclaim all liability in connection with the use of this book.

ACKNOWLEDGMENTS

Thanks to our loved ones, the Pophangover Network readers, the VGO community, and all the assholes who inspire us every day.

Published by Running Press,
An Imprint of Perseus Books, LLC,
A Subsidiary of Hachette Book Group, Inc.

Library of Congress Control Number: 2010940974

ISBN 978-0-7624-4286-7

Cover by Amanda Richmond
Edited by Jordana Tusman
Typography: GFY Handwritten Pak

Running Press Book Publishers
2300 Chestnut Street
Philadelphia, PA 19103-4371

Visit us on the web!
www.runningpress.com

CONTENTS

Dear Asshole Reading This Book,

There's no doubt about it—there are some real assholes out there. They're all around us. They're stealing our parking spaces, using their cell phones in movie theaters, holding up self-checkout lines, smelling up the office with their nasty lunches, and obsessively pushing the snooze button bright and early every morning. We all know an asshole or two. Hell, perhaps you're even an asshole yourself, but since you're reading our book, we'll let it slide. This time.

DEAR ASSHOLE is a collection of 101 uncensored, brutally honest letters to the jerks we all encounter on a daily basis. No one is safe from our wrath, from the dreaded pen thief to the asshole who didn't flush the toilet. If you've ever wanted to put these assholes in their place, or let 'em know how you really feel about their asshole-ish ways, we've got you covered.

Some people have to know they're assholes (crazy guy screaming into the Bluetooth headset, we're looking at you). Others, however, may not even be aware of how annoying they are. Getting one of these letters may be just the thing they need to open up their eyes. Some of these assholes may even change their ways, thus improving your life as a result. Just think about it: that could possibly mean no more dirty dishes in the sink, no more asshole eBay sellers, and no more assholes sweating all over the gym equipment!

We encourage you not only to read the entries, but to distribute them to offenders as you see fit. Rip them out, hand them in, mail them off, or post them up for the world to see. Let these assholes know you are on to them and aren't going to put up with their shit anymore.

Together, we can make the world a better place—one letter at a time. And, at the end of the day, is there anything more satisfying than leaving a scathing note on the windshield of the asshole who stole your parking space? We certainly don't think so.

Sincerely,
Jillian & Michelle

Dear Asshole Restaurant Server,

That was the worst service ever. You ignored me for twenty minutes before you took my order, and didn't refill my drink because you were too busy flirting with the bartender. Next time, skip the long-winded dialogue about your stupid special of the day. I came for a casual meal not to learn the sixty-two steps involved in preparing a Chilean sea bass.

Oh, and thanks for leaving my food rotting in the pickup window while you were out back smoking with the Jamaican dishwasher. That was a nice touch. Since you clearly value nicotine and dreadlocks more than hot food, I'm sure you understand why I won't be leaving you a tip.

Most sincerely,

P.S. Save the attitude. I asked you for a straw, not a kidney.
P.P.S. The bartender's just not that into you.

Dear Asshole
Restaurant Server

Dear Asshole Who Stole My Parking Space,

That was my spot, you hear me? MINE. I waited patiently with my blinker on. I made eye contact with the driver who was pulling out. We shared a moment—that special glance that says, "Yes, my spot is yours, come hither." Then, there you were, flying around the corner in your vehicle of doom, boldly pulling into my spot without a care in the world. You ruined everything. Thanks a lot, you asshole.

   (And just so you know, you probably should have parked farther back. You look like you could use the cardio.)

Warmly,

P.S. Rot in hell.

Dear Asshole Who Stole
My Parking Space

Dear Asshole Who Had This Library Book Before Me,

You're disgusting. You left crusty smears on the front cover, bite marks on the table of contents, and—dear God—did you wipe your ass with the prologue?

The whole book reeked. Cigarettes, body odor, and on page 72 I could have sworn I smelled corned beef hash. Was it absolutely vital for you to doodle dicks on every page margin? And why did you highlight that creepy passage about sacrificing chickens?

I can't possibly return the book to the librarians in this condition. Those judgmental bitches are going to think I did all of this! I'm already on their shit list from the time I ripped that dust jacket. Thanks for nothing, asshole.

Kind regards,

P.S. Toilet paper as a bookmark? Really?

Dear Asshole Who Had This
Library Book Before Me

Dear Asshole Trying to Fix Me Up,

What pathetic loser are you trying to pawn off on me now? A sweet-talking ex-con with an overbite? Your unemployed cousin who still lives in their mother's basement? Thanks, but I'll pass. Last week's candlelit dinner with the schizophrenic was the last straw. While I'll always treasure the time I spent arguing with personality No. 47, "Big Red"—a schoolgirl in Ireland with a speech impediment—I've had enough. Let me tell you, nothing quite says "romance" like discussing the potato famine over surf and turf.

Sorry, but I'm done hanging out with your parade of trolls and misfits. I don't care how "great their personality" is, either. Everyone knows that's just matchmaker-speak for "they're a total freak."

Love ya,

P.S. If they're that amazing, go out with them yourself.

Dear Asshole
Trying to Fix Me Up

C.R.A.P.

The Committe to Restrict
Asshole Performance

Dear Asshole Trying to Get in My Pants,

Back off! Just because we conversed twice doesn't
mean I want your illegitimate love child. Since
you can't seem to pick up on my subtle clues of
rejection—like me almost vomiting every time you
come near me and/or rolling my eyes every time
you open your mouth—here is a formal statement:
YOU WILL NEVER SEE WHAT'S BETWEEN MY LEGS. Or, to
put it in language your feeble mind may be better
able to understand: the chances of us becoming
intimate fall somewhere between a Teenage Mutant
Ninja Turtle being elected to the presidency and
Elvis coming back from the dead. So quit rubbing
up on me like a deprived puppy and just let it
go.

It ain't happenin',

P.S. Never.
P.P.S. EVER.

Dear Asshole Trying to
Get in My Pants

Dear Asshole Who Didn't Flush the Toilet,

Thank you so much for leaving your revolting excrement here for the world to see. It was a real treat to walk in on. I certainly hope you're feeling better, because I'm not going to be able to eat for a week.

Let me clue you in on how toilets work, you filthy, disgusting beast. First, you use them. Then, you flush them by pressing down on the HUGE SHINY HANDLE PROTRUDING OUT OF THE SIDE. I know it sounds difficult, but with a little practice I'm confident you'll be able to master it in no time.

Respectfully yours,

P.S. You may want to call a doctor. I haven't seen so many shades of neon green since Kanye West's last video.
P.P.S. Do you think you used enough toilet paper? Were you wiping, or covering a mummy?

Dear Asshole Who Didn't
Flush the Toilet

Dear Asshole at the Beach,

Turn off your radio and lower your loud mouth! I'm trying to enjoy the sounds of the ocean, and all I hear is your fat mouth gossiping to the rhythm of really bad techno. Stop shaking your towel in my direction, too. If you get one more grain of sand on me, I'll pay someone to draw a gigantic penis on your back in sunblock.

   And for the record, exactly how much food do you have in your cooler? You keep pulling stuff out of that thing like it's a clown car. Are you spending a day at the beach, or preparing for nuclear fallout?

Annoyed,

P.S. You smell like a rancid coconut.

Dear Asshole at the Beach

Dear Asshole Dentist,

Stop asking me questions while my mouth is cocked open! Sure, I'd love to tell you all about how my aunt's bridgework is holding up, but I can't form a coherent sentence with my lips wrapped around this plastic torture device. My tongue is numb and that horrid saliva vacuum is suctioning out my will to live, so forgive me if I'm not in the mood for your lame small talk. Just finish my fluoride treatment and get out of my face.

And while you're at it, update the reading material in your waiting room, you cheap bastard. I'm sick of thumbing through the same two Highlights magazines from 1987.

Mumble, mumble,

P.S. Your hygienist is a bitch.

Dear Asshole Dentist

Dear Asshole Who Keeps Pushing the Snooze Button,

I'm tired of being jolted out of semiconsciousness every nine minutes so your lazy ass can have the luxury of sleeping a few extra moments. I'm not a violent person, but your repeated snoozing has pushed me to the brink of madness. If you don't get out of bed and turn that hellish thing off, I'm going to rip it out of the wall and beat you over the head with it. How's that for a wake-up call?

And stop telling me you need to "wake up slowly." I'm not buying it. Sorry, but that excuse only works for bears coming out of hibernation.

Fondly,

P.S. Could that alarm noise be any more annoying? It sounds like an ambulance mating with a dying whale.

Dear Asshole Who Keeps
Pushing the Snooze Button

Dear Asshole Backseat Driver,

If I'm driving "too fast," it's only because I can't stand to be in the car with you any longer. You're making me nervous with your theatrics, clutching your seatbelt for dear life and slamming your foot on an imaginary brake pedal every time you want me to slow down. And that's before we've even left the driveway!

I know what I'm doing, so get off my case! Stop frantically asking me about the status of my blinker and enjoy the ride. And next time, you can drive, because I'd rather walk there than listen to one more lecture about tailgating.

Back off,

P.S. How much slower do you want me to drive? We just got passed by a fatty on a Razor scooter.

Dear Asshole Backseat Driver

Dear Asshole Always Asking Me for Favors,

It's my turn to ask a favor of you: quit asking me for fucking favors! Despite what you may think, I was not put on this earth to act as your personal servant. Start doing some things for yourself. I have my own life and it doesn't revolve around picking up your dry cleaning or painting your living room. (By the way, buttercup yellow? Really?)

Listen, Miss Daisy, go find someone else to drop your ass off at the airport. Out of curiosity, how much longer is your car going to be "in the shop," anyway? Because it's been there since Harry Potter went through puberty.

Love,

P.S. Moving again? You're on your own this time.

Dear Asshole Always
Asking Me for Favors

Dear Asshole Who Doesn't Know How to Use Self-Checkout,

Guess what? No one wants to stand around for ten minutes while you're aimlessly trying to find a bar code for your unmarked head of romaine. This is supposed to be a QUICK, CONVENIENT LANE for people who want to get in and get out. If you don't know what the hell you're doing, collect your items and take them over to Wanda in aisle four. I'm sure she'll be happy to accept your expired coupons and double-bag your kitty litter, too.

Next time, have some consideration for those of us who actually have a clue.

Good riddance,

P.S. It's an electronic signature pad, you dolt. You don't need to search your belongings for a pen.

Dear Asshole Who
Doesn't Know How to Use
Self-Checkout

Dear Overly Competitive Asshole,

I'm sick of everything turning into a game for you! Congratulations, your hemoglobin count is higher than mine. Do you want a cookie?

We can't even hang out anymore without you trying to beat me at something. No, I don't want to race you to that old oak tree or try to hold my breath longer than you. Last I checked, we weren't training for the summer Olympics, so get a fucking grip.

And for Christ's sake, we're adults. Can you please make one decision that isn't based on a game of rock, paper, scissors?

XOXO,

P.S. Blood work is not like a report card. Type A is not better than Type B, you asshole!

Dear Overly Competitive Asshole

Dear Asshole Hotel Maid,

This place is a cesspool. I found hair on the shower wall, something with six legs under the sheets, and a half-eaten stick of what I can only hope was beef jerky in the garbage can. I don't know what you're doing in here, but it's certainly not cleaning.

At the very least, grab something bristly from that squeaky cart of yours and scrub that filthy toilet. I haven't been so horrified by a bathroom since the time I walked in on my grandmother shaving her legs.

Do your job,

P.S. I know you've been snooping through my suitcase, you klepto!

Dear Asshole Hotel Maid

Dear Asshole with the Holiday Decorations Up All Year,

It's the "Twelve Days of Christmas," not the "Twelve Months of Christmas," so get that obnoxious blinking Santa off your roof. It's spring. Your wreath died weeks ago and your manger's been taken over by a family of raccoons. One can only hope baby Jesus had his rabies shot.

And while you're at it, take down those glittery ornaments and faux icicle lights. This time of year, the only things that should be boldly sparkling in the night are groups of fabulous gay men on their way to the club.

Thanks much,

P.S. There's a rosebush growing out of Frosty's ass.

Dear Asshole with
the Holiday Decorations
Up All Year

Dear Asshole Joined-at-the-Hip Couple,

Stop staring into each other's eyes for five seconds and take a look at how annoying you are. You finish each other's sentences, laugh at each other's lame jokes, and are all over each other like some sort of sick, twisted, romantically involved conjoined twins.

Live on the edge. Eat a meal alone. Go shopping by yourself. At the very least, crawl out of each other's asses long enough to go to the bathroom alone. I promise, you will not break up as a result.

Get a life,

P.S. Seek psychological help.

Dear Asshole
Joined-at-the-Hip Couple

Dear Asshole Who Bagged My Groceries,

Use paper. Use plastic. Use a Goddamn potato sack for all I care. Just stop throwing my food in there like a careless asshole. It's not rocket science. You put all the cold items together and avoid putting heavy stuff on top of fragile things. Is that too much to ask? Just once I'd like to get my bread home without it being flatter than Jillian Michaels' stomach.

And if you're going to put ninety-two canned items together, at least have the common sense to double-bag it. I'm tired of your cheap, paper-mâché bags breaking on me in the parking lot.

Much love,

P.S. Step up your game, or you'll never get promoted to that cushy cashier position.

Dear Asshole Who
Bagged My Groceries

Dear Contagious Asshole,

Excuse me, but why the hell are you here again? You've been blowing your nose for three hours straight and your nostrils are pinker than a Playboy bunny's bedroom. You should be home getting intimate with a bowl of chicken soup, not subjecting us all to whatever mutant strain of bacteria you've got coursing through your veins.

There's not enough Lysol to rid the air of whatever your last sneeze spewed out. And since I didn't wear a Level II Biohazard suit today, I'm probably going to get sick now, too. Thanks a lot, you contaminated idiot!

Concerned,

P.S. I Googled your symptoms and I think you may have the Ebola virus.
P.P.S. I hope you have good insurance.

Dear Contagious Asshole

Dear Asshole Who Works in the
Shoe Department,

Where the hell did you go? I gave you my size and you
disappeared into that little curtain-covered cubbyhole for
twenty minutes. What are you doing back there? Inventory?
Or playing footsies with your cross-eyed manager?

　　Why did you come back out with boxes stacked up to
your nose? I had no interest in seeing the same shoe in
taupe. If I wanted to see the fucking shoe in taupe, I would
have asked to see it in taupe, you asshole!

　　And for the record, I know the shoe fits fine. I'm
wearing it. I don't need you to slam your fat thumb down
on my big toe to prove it to me.

Peace out,

P.S. Is that a shoehorn in your pocket or are you just
happy to see me?

Dear Asshole Who Works
in the Shoe Department

Dear Asshole Houseguest Who Overstayed Your Welcome,

You said you just needed a place to crash while you got back on your feet. Exactly how much longer is that going to take, because you're driving me crazy. My couch has a permanent impression of your ass in it, and you've single-handedly ruined my love life. You've been here so long my mailman thinks we're fucking.

   If you're not going to pay me rent or pick up after yourself, at least have the decency to close the door when you're in the bathroom. I could have gone to my grave without seeing you wipe your ass last week.

Always,

P.S. Now you're messing with my Netflix queue?! That's the last straw.
P.P.S. The Horse Whisperer? Really??

Dear Asshole Houseguest
Who Overstayed Your Welcome

Dear Asshole Who Keeps Showing Up Without Calling,

I'm inside trying to get things done, and you're out there banging on my door like a Jehovah's Witness on crack. What the hell is your problem? We're adults. We're not Seinfeld characters. You can't just show up on a whim every time you're bored or want a snack. I have a life of my own and I'm not going to drop everything I was doing just because you were "in the neighborhood."

Next time, call me before you decide to start invading my privacy and hovering outside my door like a stalker. Forgive me, but I'm just not in the mood for one of your impromptu games of Twister. I'm not seven. I have things to do.

Ciao,

P.S. Don't bother knocking again, asshole. I'm ignoring you.

Dear Asshole Who Keeps
Showing Up Without Calling

Dear Asshole Who Stole My Pen,

You've crossed the line. Pen theft is a serious crime. Do you have any idea what I had to go through to get that thing? Pens don't grow on trees, you know.

Sure, other pens may come along, but they won't have that smooth gliding rollerball or contoured comfort grip. Gone are the days of my colorful translucent plastic barrel basking in the fluorescent light. You've stripped that joy from me. Have you no soul?

That was MY pen, you hear me? Mine!

FU,

P.S. See you in hell.

Dear Asshole
Who Stole My Pen

Dear Asshole Graffiti "Artist,"

I don't know what the hell you think you painted, but it looks like a twelve-foot mural of a Cosby sweater. What's with all the random letters? I can't tell if you tagged your gang at the end or had a seizure while holding the paint can.

Don't get me wrong. I'm impressed you found the time to decorate a wall between your hectic schedule of detention and drug use, but you need to find another hobby. We're all tired of looking at your girlfriend's name. If you love her so much, go hang out with her instead of ruining the neighborhood with your tacky aerosol declarations, you asshole.

Thanks bunches,

P.S. For a tough guy, you sure do seem to love the color pink.

Dear Asshole
Graffiti "Artist"

Dear Asshole Who Broke into My Car,

By now, you've surely realized I don't keep any important stuff in my vehicle. That's so scumbag assholes like you won't walk away with anything valuable. Tell me, what is the black market value of a half-eaten pack of gum and a scratched Madonna CD these days?

I'm terribly sorry my belongings couldn't subsidize an exquisite evening of heavy drug use for you and your degenerate friends, but I hope I have instead provided you with hours of wholesome entertainment via my tantalizing music collection and original-flavored Big League Chew.

Au revoir,

P.S. I had a pen on the dash. You could at least have written me a thank-you note.
P.P.S. You break glass like a girl.

Dear Asshole Who
Broke into My Car

Dear Asshole Who Borrowed My Shirt,

I don't know what the hell you did to this thing, but you have some nerve giving it back to me in this condition. It's stretched out and it's completely covered with holes and stains. Did you spend the night playing rugby in a cactus patch or did you just get frisky with your cheese grater?

   Don't even get me started on the horrific odor permeating the fabric, either. Did you happen to encounter a decomposing body at any time in the last twenty-four hours? Sure smells like it. You could at least have washed it, or in this extreme case, just burned it and told me it was lost.

You owe me.

P.S. No, you can't borrow my new jeans, you asshole!

Dear Asshole Who Borrowed My Shirt

Dear Asshole Who Left the Shopping
Cart in the Middle of the Parking Lot,

Would it have killed you to walk the extra three
feet to the cart return, you lazy sloth? Now your
carriage is aimlessly floating around the parking
lot like a tumbleweed in a bad country music video
and it could end up damaging someone's car.

   I understand you were probably in a rush to get
back to the rat-infested double-wide trailer you
call home, but that doesn't give you the right to
act like an inconsiderate slob. Put the cart back
when you're done with it. And take those nasty
crumpled tissues you left in it with you, too.

Have a great day,

P.S. EVERYONE HATES YOU!

Dear Asshole Who Left the Shopping Cart in the Middle of the Parking Lot

Dear Asshole Landlord,

Congratulations on officially achieving slumlord status with this place, because it's a total shithole. The paint is peeling, the windows won't open, and the furnace is smoking more than the cast of Mad Men. Does someone need to die an asbestos-related death before you'll even return a phone call?

   If you're not going to call me back, at least tell me who I have to screw around here for a hot shower. The water is freezing. I'm trying to freshen up before work, not reduce a deadly fever.

Miserably yours,

P.S. Doorknobs are not a luxury.

Dear Asshole Landlord

Dear Asshole at the Laundromat,

In case you didn't get the memo, this isn't a storage facility. It's a Laundromat. You don't get to leave your nasty clothes rotting in the washing machine for three hours while you're off gallivanting around town. When the machine cycle ends, get your belongings out of my way. I need to wash my clothes, too, and there's no way in hell I'm touching your intimate apparel without wearing a full-body condom.

And by the way, that's a laundry cart, not an ottoman. Get your fat ass off it so people can transport their wet laundry.

Get a clue,

P.S. Your whites look really dingy. Ever hear of bleach?

Dear Asshole at
the Laundromat

Dear Cheapskate Asshole,

The jig is up, you miserly, penny-pinching Scrooge! We all know you aren't poor, so stop acting like the repo men are coming for your possessions every time a bill is due. There's more to life than accumulating a financial nest egg, so take that stick out of your tightwad ass and live a little. Stop wrapping gifts in newspaper. Buy a color television. Hell go crazy and pick up a new roll of aluminum foil instead of using that same little wrinkled piece over and over.

And by the way, how old is your car? That thing has seen better days. It's sort of like Pamela Anderson, only without the airbags. Safety first!

Toodles,

P.S. No, you're not eligible for food stamps, you asshole!

Dear Cheapskate Asshole

Dear Asshole Who Won't Stop for Directions,

Just admit it: we're lost! We've been driving around in circles for so long that I'm starting to feel dizzy. I now know these streets better than my own neighborhood, and we've cruised by that bank so many times the employees probably think we're planning a robbery.

    I actually have a life outside this vehicle, so stop being such a stubborn asshole and pull into a gas station for directions. And while you're at it, buy me a soda. All that gasping and fearing for my life while driving through that last ghetto made my mouth a bit dry.

Yours,

P.S. I could have crawled there faster than this!

Dear Asshole Who Won't
Stop for Directions

Dear Asshole Clean Freak,

What the hell is wrong with you? Have all those Pledge fumes finally gone to your head? It's one thing to be neat and tidy, but you've taken it way too far. Your kitchen is sparkling, and if your bathroom gets any more sterile, surgeons could start using it as an operating room. So put down the cleaning bucket and step away from the Swiffer. And stop shooting me looks of death because the tip of my shoe accidentally touched the edge of the coffee table.

    For the record, the only person who should be that obsessed with removing fingerprints is a forensic analyst. Last I checked, you didn't work in CSI, so lighten up a little.

Onward and upward,

P.S. You missed a spot.

Dear Asshole Clean Freak

Dear Asshole Who Smelled Up the Elevator,

Didn't you get the memo? Passing gas in tiny, confined spaces is NOT OKAY. I don't know what you've been eating that could possibly have caused such a toxic odor, but by the third floor, my eyes were watering. And by the fifth, I started welcoming death.

I shouldn't need a SARS mask to get to my destination because of your gastrointestinal issues, you asshole. Next time, act like a civilized human being. Hold it in instead of making strangers suffer in your noxious, gaseous misery.

Stay away,

P.S. Don't even try to blame the elderly woman in the corner. I know it was you.

Dear Asshole Who Smelled Up the Elevator

Dear Constantly Broke Asshole,

You seriously have got to do something about your cash-flow problem, because being friends with you is like being whisked away on a hellish journey back to 1802. The activities we can enjoy together have been reduced to playing hopscotch, making shadow puppets, and telling ghostly tales by the campfire. I'm really over it. Get a better job. Play a saxophone near the transit system. Pawn off some of your ugly jewelry. Anything! Because if I have to spend one more night sitting around listening to you complaining about your maxed-out credit cards, I'll go insane.

Your friend,

P.S. Did you really just put $1.73 worth of gas in your car?

Dear Constantly Broke Asshole

Dear Conceited Asshole,

The world doesn't revolve around you, so get over yourself. You're unreasonable, selfish, and require more doting and attention than an endangered baby panda. For Christ's sake, can't you put your cell phone camera down for five seconds? I think we've all seen enough photos of you flashing a duck face in a bathroom mirror. Besides, we all know the truth: you're overcompensating because inside you're barren and empty, sort of like a theater showing a Dane Cook movie.

At least I'll know where to find you when the world ends—in the mirror applying gel to the top of your head.

Take a hike,

P.S. You're so vain, you probably think this letter's about you.
P.P.S. Okay, fine. This time it is, you asshole.

Dear Conceited Asshole

Dear Asshole Debbie Downer,

Chill out with the tragic statistics and morbid topics of conversation. No one wants to hear how many kittens died last year from feline AIDS, or how much your irritable bowel acts up when you eat spicy foods. Enough already! You're putting everyone in a bad mood!

The last time I heard you say something positive, it was that you were "positive" something horrible was going to happen. Pop a Prozac or two, because you're so depressed, the glass isn't half empty; it's broken and you want to cut yourself with it.

Faithfully yours,

P.S. Thanks, but I don't need a ten-minute soliloquy on hurricane fatalities every time it rains.

Dear Asshole Debbie Downer

Dear Asshole Litterer,

The world outside of your car window is not a garbage receptacle. You can't just throw your beer bottles and fast food bags out there and expect someone else to clean up after you, you slob. What's your issue? There are garbage cans all over the place. You know, those rare and elusive cylindrical devices that can be found on almost every street corner? Start using them, because if I see one more Combos wrapper floating whimsically across my lawn, someone will lose an eye.

Bite me,

P.S. You better dispose of this letter properly, asshole.

Dear Asshole Litterer

Dear Asshole Mean Drunk,

Liquor is not your friend. Every time you drink, you turn into an aggressive dickhead and everyone's tired of dealing with your booze-infused rages. Sorry, but my idea of a fun night doesn't involve watching you punching walls or threatening to castrate the DJ. Yes, I know Taylor Swift dance remixes suck harder than a $2 hooker, but sometimes you just have to let it go.

Do the world a favor: put down that penny well drink and back away slowly. Because the next time you pick a fight with a four-hundred-pound ex-con, you're on your own.

Bottoms up,

P.S. It's a mannequin! It wasn't "trying to start shit" with you!

Dear Asshole Mean Drunk

Dear Asshole Weatherman on TV,

Are you even a real meteorologist, or are you just some douchebag who got the job because your daddy's a producer? Your forecasts are always way off the mark. Either your little Doppler 9000 is a piece of shit, or you simply have no clue. Do you even know what all those colors and squiggly lines mean, or are you just standing in front of that screen with your little Jeopardy clicker winging it?

Enough with the fear-mongering, too. Every day you're running off your mouth about another "dangerous weather system moving in from the south" Bitch, please. I've seen more wind and rain in a Lady Gaga video than in one of your so called "storms," so give it a rest.

Go back to school,

P.S. You have a face for radio.

Dear Asshole
Weatherman on TV

Dear Asshole Lifeguard,

I see you over there, pacing back and forth with your little red buoy like you're the world's most influential authority on water safety. Get over yourself. I'm not breaking any of your stupid rules, so take your bottle of white zinc oxide and your stack of Baywatch DVDs and go lecture the toddlers in the kiddie area.

You may want to hit the gym while you're at it. You weigh one hundred pounds. How is your puny ass even going to rescue anything, anyway? Unless a horseshoe crab is struggling with a rip current, I doubt you'll be any help.

Cheerio,

P.S. Stop blowing that whistle!
P.P.S. You can't run in slow motion, so don't even try.

Dear Asshole
Lifeguard

Dear Asshole Gossiper,

Psst: have you heard the latest buzz on the street? It's that everyone thinks you're an annoying wench. I'm tired of you whispering nonsense in my face every five seconds. I've got my own life to worry about. I don't care who so-and-so is blowing, or that my neighbor buys their underwear at Big Lots. Besides, most of your boring stories aren't even true. I hate to burst your bubble, but "a little birdie" is not a reputable source of information unless you want an honest opinion on seed.

Aloha,

P.S. You didn't hear this from me.

Dear Asshole Gossiper

Dear Constantly Cheery Asshole,

You're not spreading joy, you're making us want to kill ourselves with your forced positivity and your phony perma-grin. Message received: you love life and you shit Technicolor rainbows. Now hop into a Crock-Pot and simmer down, because you're at a ten and we need you at a four. You're acting deranged, doodling smiley faces on things and skipping around like a hyperactive child who just overdosed on Pixy Stix. Life isn't that grand all the time, so put your unicorn pillowcases in storage and join the rest of us in the real world.

Regretfully,

P.S. Ease off on the red pills.

Dear Constantly
Cheery Asshole

Dear Asshole Practical Joker,

Grow up, you attention-seeking clown. Your little stunts aren't even funny; they're just plain lame. Wow, you put my mouse in a Jell-O mold and changed my screensaver to a fat woman in a bikini. How hilarious!

Not only are your pranks devoid of humor, they have crossed the threshold into being a pure annoyance. Nothing says "fun" like scrubbing Silly String stains out of my couch, or spending the afternoon popping all of your stupid pornographic balloon creations. Not only were those activities time-consuming, but now everyone thinks I'm a pervert.

Boo,

P.S. If you need a quarter that badly, I'll give you one. Leave my ear out of it.
P.P.S. I'm not sure what you think a penis looks like, but that wasn't it.

Dear Asshole Practical Joker

Dear Asshole Celebrity,

No, I'm not writing for your autograph or to request an 8x10 glossy photo of your bloated head. I really just wanted to call you an asshole.

Wow, you're famous and people know your name. That doesn't give you an all-access pass to act like an egotistical douchebag. Who do you think you are, sashaying around town with your oversized cataract sunglasses and your entourage of thirty overweight men? Morph into a Kit Kat and give me a break.

I'm sure a million people tell you how fabulous you are every day, but I'm not going to bow down to some loser who dropped out of high school and used to stock shelves at Woolworth's just because some Hollywood asshole thought you had "the look." Yeah, you have the look all right—the look of someone who belongs in rehab.

Arrivederci,

P.S. I heard Julia Roberts hates you.

Dear Asshole Celebrity

Dear Asshole Flight Attendant,

Eight weeks at the flight academy
and you still don't know how to pour
a soda amidst light turbulence? Wow,
I wish I'd known that before I
ordered a beverage, because now it's
all over me. No, I don't want your
grody lukewarm towel or your pack of
seven stale peanuts, so stop
scraping my knee every five minutes
with your rickety cart.
   My seatbelt is fastened and my
tray is in the folded position, so
give it a rest. And while you're at
it, stop rolling your eyes at my
carry-on. It's regulation size, you
phony plastic bitch.

Fly the friendly skies,

P.S. You'll never marry a pilot.

Dear Asshole Flight Attendant

Dear Asshole Gamer,

You probably lack the attention span to read this, but somewhere in that Mountain Dew-infused brain of yours, I know there is a hero. After all you've slain dragons, saved princesses, and restored order to war-torn lands. While you may be "totally epic" in Stormwind City, here in the real world you're just a lazy, disillusioned asshole with a hygiene problem. Judging by the smell coming off your body, you haven't showered since Mario and Luigi were still in the womb. Word to the wise: you can shut out the world, but you can't run from head lice.

And another thing: stop screaming into your headset and acting like a whiny little bitch every time someone snipes you from the bushes. Face it: if you didn't suck at the game, that wouldn't have happened.

Always yours,

P.S. Have you gained weight?

Dear Asshole Gamer

Dear Asshole Sports Fanatic,

Sit down and watch the game instead of foaming at the mouth like a rabid maniac every time your team fumbles the ball. News flash: the players can't hear your stupid coaching advice, so shut the hell up and save us all the aggravation. If you want to do something productive, go strip off some of that team apparel. You're covered in more tacky embroidery than my grandmother's favorite quilt.

Save your useless statistics, too. If I wanted to hear boring stories about people getting to third base, I'd go hang out at a college fraternity.

Rah rah sis-boom-bah,

P.S. They'll never get a championship ring.

Dear Asshole Sports Fanatic

Dear Asshole at the Movie Theater,

Turn your cell phone off and enjoy the movie! I didn't pay $20 to watch you texting with your degenerate friends, so give it a rest. Besides, I can't focus on Jude Law's receding hairline with that blinding light raping my retinas every fifteen seconds.

It's bad enough that I have to endure your cell phone laser show, but I certainly can't hear anything over your bag crinkling, cow chomping, or cackling hyena laugh either. And seriously, stop getting up. I'm tired of giving myself a charley horse every time your fat ass has to squeeze through the aisle. If your bladder is the size of a quarter, perhaps you should just opt for DVDs at home instead.

All the best,

P.S. Unless you're having an epileptic seizure or need medical attention, stop kicking my chair!

Dear Asshole at the Movie Theater

Dear Online Dating Asshole Who
Lied About Their Looks,

You said you looked like a Greek god. I
guess you forgot to mention that the god
was missing four teeth and needed a
boomerang to put on a belt. Why did you
check "weight lifter" under body type?
The only things you've been lifting are
french fries and Paula Deen cookbooks.
  And seriously, how old is that photo
you're using in your profile? When you said
"twenties," I thought you were referring to
your age, not the decade the picture was
taken.

LOL,

P.S. Zeus and Aphrodite didn't have acne.

Dear Online Dating Asshole
Who Lied About Their Looks

Dear Asshole Bad Kisser,

Making out is supposed to be fun, not torture. One minute you're slobbering all over my face like a basset hound, and the next you're hoovering my lips off like a vacuum. Calm down. You're kissing me, not trying to suction venom out of a snakebite.

    Loosen up a little. Your body is so stiff, it feels like rigor mortis has started to set in. And stop darting your lizard tongue in and out of my mouth, too. It's not turning me on, it's triggering my gag reflex.

Ew.

P.S. Teeth are NOT OKAY.
P.P.S. If you try to lick my eyelid again, I will murder you.

Dear Asshole Bad Kisser

Dear Asshole Gym Sweater,

Wipe down the equipment when you're done with it, you disgusting sweaty pig! You could fill an Olympic-sized swimming pool with the amount of perspiration you left on this machine. Paper towels and disinfectant are your friend. Use them. Because, trust me when I say no one here wants to see a sweaty imprint of your robust ass cheeks.

Your profuse sweating is interfering with my gym experience. The free weights are gross and moist, and you've single-handedly turned the treadmill into a Slip 'n Slide. Invest in some terrycloth bands, or just buy a Thighmaster and work out at home.

Burn baby burn,

P.S. You may want to pay a little more attention to your calves.

Dear Asshole Gym Sweater

Dear Asshole Phony Psychic,

Did I really just pay you forty bucks to tickle my hand and tell me I have a dead relative? Give me a break! I want my money back, you fraud!

Yes, I eat food every day. And yes, my name DOES have a vowel in it (how ever did you know?)! Look, just cut to the chase, Miss Cleo. I've been here for fifteen minutes already and I'm not getting any younger. Spare me the generic bullshit and tell me something I don't know, like whether Saturday Night Live will ever be funny again.

Thanks for nothing,

P.S. Your tarot cards must be broken, because I've never had a pet rat named Lewis.
P.P.S. That's not even a crystal ball. It's a spray-painted coconut. I'm not an idiot.

Dear Asshole
Phony Psychic

Dear Asshole Wearing Too Much Fragrance,

Ever wonder why people maintain that permanent ten-foot radius around you? It's because you reek, and no one wants to be trapped in your overpowering cloud of stench. Fragrances are supposed to be sexy and subtle. They're not supposed to cause asphyxiation, you smelly asshole!

Next time, don't douse yourself in six bottles of that toilet water before you leave the house. My throat is closing up, I can barely breathe, and my eyes haven't teared up this much since I watched Marley and Me (spoiler alert: the damn dog died, okay?).

P-fucking-U,

P.S. You're literally a walking, talking biochemical weapon.

Dear Asshole Wearing
Too Much Fragrance

Dear Asshole Who Parked Like a Moron,

Congratulations! That's the worst parking job I've ever seen. I don't know how you managed to cram your hideous car into such a small spot, but it truly is a sight to behold.

    Here's a little tip for you: parking spaces are like coloring books. You're supposed to stay within the lines. You can't just go around ignoring other cars and boxing people in like you own the place. This isn't the Dukes of Hazzard and I'm not driving the General Lee. I shouldn't have to perform a fucking window stunt to enter my vehicle because you parked like a douchebag.

Truly,

P.S. I know we all learn how to drive in parking lots, but your stupid ass must have been born in one, too.

Dear Asshole Who
Parked Like a Moron

Dear Asshole Goody Two-Shoes,

I'm sick to death of you and your brown-nosing, holier-than-thou ways. Get over yourself! I'm thrilled that you enjoy sitting home all day perfecting your penmanship and coming up with lame alternatives for curse words, but don't chastise me because I don't want to join you. And it's not because I'm a morally corrupt person with no values, either. It's because you're a judgmental bitch who doesn't know how to have any fun.

Oh, and spare me the constant lectures about my "sinful" lifestyle. Calm down, Laura Ingalls Wilder. I had two beers on a Thursday night. You don't need to stage an intervention.

Eat it,

P.S. I know you were the one who deleted all the Tupac songs from my iTunes library.

Dear Asshole
Goody Two-Shoes

Dear Asshole with the Spray Tan,

I know you think being that hideous color makes you look sexy, but sadly, it just makes you look like a rejected cast member from Jersey Shore. Really, though, the only "situation" going on in your world is that your neon face is visible from the Russian space station.

    I hate to break it to you, but "pumpkin orange" isn't an acceptable skin color for human beings. You're an obsessed tanorexic and you've taken things way too far. You don't have a healthy sun-kissed glow. You look like a radioactive Oompa Loompa.

Give it up,

P.S. At least apply it evenly. Your face is covered with more stripes than the American flag.

Dear Asshole with
the Spray Tan

Dear Asshole Roommate,

I'm trying to sleep. If you and your heartbroken loser friends don't stop karaoking to "I Will Survive," I'm going to come out there and ensure that you won't. Here's a thought: why don't you stop butchering inspirational disco tunes and go clean up your mess? Your shit is piled up everywhere and this place is starting to look like an episode of Hoarders.

And while I have your ear, so help me God, if you "accidentally" unplug my coffeemaker one more time, there will be blood.

Bye-bye,

P.S. Back the fuck off my organic crackers.
P.P.S. You got dumped because you're annoying.

Dear Asshole Roommate

Dear Asshole Whistler,

I can't see you, but I know you're there. I can hear your ear-piercing nasal gymnastics bellowing through the atmosphere from a mile away. Aren't your lips tired yet? You've been tweeting those same three notes for the past ten minutes. Give it a rest. You're giving me a migraine and you're driving all the dogs in the neighborhood totally insane.

If you are going to whistle loud enough for everyone in the vicinity to hear, at least make it a modern, recognizable tune. Frankly, I can't tell if you're reprising a show tune or trying to get that canary to mate with you.

Zip-a-dee-doo-dah,

P.S. There's a special place in hell reserved for people like you.

Dear Asshole Whistler

Dear Asshole Foodie,

Shut up and eat your dinner. You're not Julia Child, and no one is interested in enduring a detailed analysis about what hints of exotic spice your delicate palate was able to detect in the chutney mayo. The only thing you are an aficionado of is how to be annoying.

And for the love of God, please stop with all the nauseating noises and facial theatrics. We get it. Your meal tastes good. You don't need to launch a full-blown foodgasm after every bite to convince us.

Thanks,

P.S. Stop playing twenty questions with the restaurant server and just order your food already, you pretentious prick!

Dear Asshole Foodie

Dear Lotto-Playing Asshole Holding Up the Line,

Shouldn't you have come prepared with your magical winning picks instead of standing there at the machine mumbling random number sequences like some rain man with a gambling problem? Here, I have some numbers for you: 4-1-1. Dial them and get a clue, because you aren't going to win.

And while you're at it, take your little scratch-off tickets and move your ass to the back of the line. I'll be damned if I'm going to stand here twiddling my thumbs for fifteen minutes while you're feverishly trying to match up three jeweled treasure boxes.

Jackpot,

P.S. Just buy a Quick Pick and get out of my face already!

Dear Lotto-Playing Asshole
Holding Up the Line

Dear Asshole Psychotic Ex,

We're not together anymore, so quit harassing me.
I've moved on with my life and I really think you
should do the same. Besides, there are plenty of
other fish in the sea that you can latch your
depressed hooks into and make miserable. I've
done my time.

   Unless you want the cops called on your ass,
stop driving by my house all slow in the middle of
the night. I know it's you, you stalker freak. I'd
recognize the rumble of your busted muffler
anywhere. And while you're at it, stop calling me
from that "private" number, too. You're not fooling
anyone. It's obviously either you or that creepy guy
from India who keeps trying to sell me that
collection of Bicentennial coins. Either way, I'm not
going to answer.

Hatefully,

P.S. I see you hiding behind that bush.
P.P.S. Dear God, are you wearing my underwear?
P.P.P.S. ON YOUR HEAD?

Dear Asshole Psychotic Ex

Dear Asshole at the Concert,

Guess what? I didn't pay $100 for this ticket to hear some busted, losery drunk screaming off-pitch lyrics in my ear the whole night. You're ruining the show! And you're not even singing the right words! I've listened to this song a hundred times and I know for a fact it doesn't reference a pimp on a unicycle, so learn the lyrics or shut the fuck up.

I'd appreciate it if you'd stop air-guitaring all up in my personal space, too. Consider yourself warned. If your sweaty arm slimes me one more time, I'll wrap that invisible whammy bar around your neck.

Shhhhhh,

P.S. You suck harder than the opening act.
P.P.S. Put down the lighter. Don't be that guy.

Dear Asshole at the Concert

Dear Asshole Acquaintance Who Invited Me to Their Wedding,

Here's my RSVP: I won't be attending your boring nuptials or tacky reception. I HARDLY KNOW YOU. We conversed about the weather once in 1998. That doesn't mean I want to watch you and your deadbeat fiancé doing the chicken dance till dawn. Sorry, but there's absolutely no incentive for me to show up. Everyone knows you're too cheap to pay for an open bar, and if you've eaten one disgusting slab of catered prime rib, you've eaten them all.

Looks like you're gonna have to find another sucker to buy you that stainless steel cappuccino maker from your registry.

Good luck,

P.S. I give you guys three months. Max.

Dear Asshole Acquaintance Who
Invited Me to Their Wedding

Dear Asshole IT Guy,

Just because you took a two-week course on the Microsoft Word suite doesn't mean you get to walk around here patronizing the rest of us, you asshole. Yes, I rebooted my computer and cleared my cookies. I'm not a moron. So march your geeky ass back to your World of Warcraft-decorated cubicle and find me a real solution to my problem.

And don't install any more antivirus software on my computer, either. It's already slow enough. At this point, my C drive is more heavily protected than the sacred remains of King Tut.

Control-Alt-Delete this,

P.S. No, my mouse is not unplugged!
P.P.S. If you mutter the word "cache" again, you will lose a testicle.

Dear Asshole IT Guy

Dear Asshole Hairdresser,

You totally butchered my hair. The back is uneven and my bangs look like they were bitten off by Hannibal Lecter. At this point, I'm thinking Stevie Wonder could have done a better job with hedge clippers and some mousse.

Thanks for burning my scalp in that deathtrap you call a sink, too. I honestly don't know which was more painful: the scalding water, or listening to you talk about your alcoholic fiancé's STD. At least my burns will heal, which is more than I can say about your genitals.

And by the way, you can say "a little to the left" as much as you want. This is as far as my head turns. I'm not an owl.

Snip snip,

P.S. I should have known better; your hair's more feathered than a Canada Goose.

Dear Asshole Hairdresser

Dear Asshole Cyclist,

This isn't the Tour de France, so get your sweaty ass out of the middle of the road. Cars are swerving dangerously to avoid you, and I shouldn't have to die because you're obsessed with bulking up your puny calves.

Exactly how aerodynamic do you need to be, you narcissistic prick? That skintight rainbow spandex suit isn't making you navigate the neighborhood any faster. It's just making you look like a douche.

And seriously, stop flashing those spastic hand signals at me. I can't tell if you're swatting at a bug or preparing to take that left onto Sycamore.

Cheers,

P.S. You will never be Lance Armstrong, so just quit while you're ahead.

Dear Asshole Cyclist

Dear Asshole Mailman,

You lazy postal piece of shit! I leave you a bottle of
re-gifted wine every year in the hopes that you'll
at least walk the four feet to my front door when
I get a package that won't fit into my mailbox, but
you can't even be bothered to do that. Instead, you
just sit there in your cushy government-supported
buggy pretending to sort mail for hours at a
time—I'm on to you. I know what you're really doing
in there is just finger-fucking everybody's mail to
get the latest neighborhood gossip.

   (No. I didn't get into Yale. But thanks for
caring.)

Return to sender,

P.S. I order that catalog for my friend. Don't
judge me!

Dear Asshole Mailman

Dear Asshole Ordering Eight Beverages in Front of Me at the Coffee Shop,

Oh how I loathe seeing you standing there in front of me with your long list of specialty orders, trying to look inconspicuous while feigning interest in that Norah Jones CD. It takes a long time to make a blended coffee beverage—and you just ordered eight! Now I have to stand around with my thumb up my ass for the next twenty-five minutes, shifting my gaze between the barista's latest piercing and a selection of tacky, overpriced earthenware mugs, just so your lazy coworkers can get their caffeine fix. Bullshit!

Thanks for ruining my few precious moments of break time. Here's hoping you hit a pothole on your way back to work and spill coffee all over your ugly cloth interior.

You suck,

P.S. No one's going to pay you back.
P.P.S. You're being used.

Dear Asshole Ordering
Eight Beverages in Front of
Me at the Coffee Shop

Dear Asshole with the Bluetooth,

When I first saw you walking toward me talking to yourself, I thought you were crazy. Then I saw that ridiculous Bluetooth jutting out of the side of your bloated head and realized you were just an arrogant prick. Tell me, does wearing that oversized hearing aid everywhere you go make you feel special? Because to the rest of us, it doesn't scream "success and importance." It just screams "I had twenty dollars."

And by the way, the microphone is sensitive. YOU DON'T HAVE TO SCREAM INTO IT LIKE A LUNATIC. You're in public, for Christ's sake! Spare the world the details of your recent colonoscopy and talk at a normal volume.

Over and out,

P.S. Can you hear me now?

Dear Asshole with
the Bluetooth

Dear Asshole Who Didn't Clean Up After Their Dog,

I don't know what you've been feeding that pet of yours, but it just left a pile of human-sized turds in the middle of the sidewalk. Guess what? This isn't Fido's personal toilet, you asshole! It's a public sidewalk and no one in the neighborhood wants to walk by, inhale, step in, or otherwise interact with his shit. It's time for you to embrace the responsibilities of pet ownership. Attach some plastic baggies to your hand. Buy yourself a pooper scooper. Anything. Because the next time you fail to clean up after your dog's dump, I'm going to follow you home and smear it on your pillow. Comprende?

Smooches,

P.S. Cesar Millan called. He said you were an asshole.

Dear Asshole Who
Didn't Clean Up After Their Dog

Dear Asshole Dressing Room Attendant,

Stop knocking on my door every five seconds asking me if I'm okay. Of course I'm okay! I'm in here trying on some jeans, not disarming a bomb.

No, I don't need a bigger size, another color, or a different fit. What I need is for you to stop lurking outside my door so I can take off my pants in peace. Give me some space, you perv! I see you trying to get a glimpse of my bare torso through that slotted door! Don't you have some hangers to organize or something?

Better yet, run along and learn to count, since you gave me a ticket for six items and I really have nine.

Later,

P.S. I know you're still out there. I can hear you breathing.

Dear Asshole Dressing
Room Attendant

Dear Asshole Soft Talker,

I've leaned in. I've concentrated. I've squinted my eyes. I've prayed to the patron saint of Helen Keller. But I still can't hear a single word coming out of your fucking mouth! I'm not a lip reader, so quit mumbling under your breath like a meek schoolgirl and speak up already. Just once, I'd like to have a conversation that doesn't involve me nodding my head and saying "what, what" every two seconds, like I'm Puff Daddy laying down background vocals on a new track. Is that too much to ask?

Sincerely,

P.S. (inaudible mumbling)

Dear Asshole
Soft Talker

Dear Asshole Who Left Their Garage
Sale Sign Up for Three Months,

I'm sick and tired of seeing your ugly,
tattered neon signs flapping in the wind!
Your little yard sale ended weeks ago, so get
off your lazy ass and take those stupid
things down. They're not doing anything but
uglifying the neighborhood and confusing
people. They're not even legible! The ink is
so smeared, I can't tell if you're inviting me
over to buy your junk, or boldly proclaiming
your love for the eldest Jonas brother.
   Besides, I went to one of your little
shindigs and your crap was way overpriced.
Twenty-five bucks for a broken Lite-Brite?
Really?

Leave town,

P.S. Try Craigslist.

Dear Asshole Who Left
Their Garage Sale Sign Up
for Three Months

Dear Asshole Stalking
My Blog,

I'm thrilled that you find me so
interesting, but you've officially
crossed the line between "casual reader"
and "total weirdo." I know you spend
your days spam-refreshing my blog every
fifteen seconds waiting for a new post
and you get your jollies by leaving
creepy comments under all those fake
names.

   The game is over! I can see your IP
address, you idiot! There's no anonymity
on the Internet and my stats tracker
doesn't lie! So back off, you unstable
little troll. Quit tracking me like Dog
the Bounty Hunter and find yourself a
new hobby.

Seek psychological help,

P.S. Did you really just spend forty-two
minutes staring at my new photo, you
sicko?

Dear Asshole Stalking My Blog

Dear Social Media-Obsessed Asshole,

This is getting out of hand. Yesterday, you Tweeted your friends on Myspace about the YouTube video on your Tumblr blog. Why did you send me a virtual banana on Facebook? I see you every day.

The last time we went out to eat, you spent more time taking photos of your meal than actually eating it. No one needs a seven-page spread of your peanut butter on rye. You're sharing too much. At this point, your "friend" in Croatia knows more about your ass than your proctologist. Is nothing sacred?

Poke,

P.S. I unfriended you this morning.

Dear Social Media-
Obsessed Asshole

Dear Asshole with the
Body Odor,

I'm going to let you in on a little secret:
YOU REEK. The odors emanating from your
body are mind-numbingly, gut-wrenchingly,
plant-wiltingly bad. I'm serious when I say
you smell like a fucking curry factory.
    What the hell is wrong with your nose? Has
it become completely desensitized to your
putrid stench, or do you just get some sick
pleasure out of making people throw up in
their mouths?
    Do the world a favor: go get reacquainted
with some soap and water because you smell
like you haven't bathed since the Ming
dynasty ruled China. Confucius says, "P.U.!"

Good luck with that,

P.S. You may want to burn that shirt.

Dear Asshole with
the Body Odor

Dear Asshole at the ATM,

How much longer are you going to stand there fumbling at the machine? I could have watched the complete Star Wars box set in the time it's taken you to check your balance. What's the issue? I'd like to get $40 out of my account before inflation makes it totally worthless.
   And by the way, there's no need to pull a muscle, twisting and turning your back to shield the keypad. Calm down. I'm not trying to catch a glimpse of your PIN number. We all know it's just your birth date, anyway.

Use the force,

P.S. ATM doesn't stand for Asshole at the Teller Machine, so hurry the fuck up!

Dear Asshole at the ATM

Dear Pussywhipped Asshole,

You used to be a cool guy. What the hell happened to you? We don't even hang out anymore because you're too busy picking out ceramic cats and spooning to Gilmore Girls reruns. It's bad, man. Last week, you bought a Josh Groban CD and actually used the word "scrapbooking."

Face it: she's got your balls in a paisley-colored vise grip. You cater to her every whim on the off chance it will earn you a mediocre blow job, and it's pathetic.

Have fun hosting your little pedicure parties and making scented candles. If you ever get tired of that bullshit, you know where to find us.

Hasta la vista, baby,

P.S. Did you ask her permission before reading this letter?

Dear Pussywhipped Asshole

Dear Asshole Who Brought
Seafood to Work,

This whole office smells like a mermaid's
vagina and it's all your fault. I'm not sure
what sort of sea life you're eating over
there, but it smells like it was caught during
the Reagan administration.

Your rancid meals are ruining my life. I
can't use the microwave anymore because
everything comes out infused with your
nasty seafood medley, and I go home every
night smelling like I just worked a twelve-
hour shift on a crab boat. Enough is
enough! If I wanted to spend eight hours
breathing in the foul scents of low tide, I'd
go to New Jersey.

Warm wishes,

P.S. Your microwave popcorn reeks, too.

Dear Asshole Who
Brought Seafood to Work

Dear Asshole Bartender,

Are you blind? I've been standing here waving this $20 bill in the air for ten minutes! Stop flirting with the underage jailbait in the corner and take my drink order. I'd like to get a buzz on before I die of old age. And lose the attitude, pal. Just because you get to stand behind a counter in fancy suspenders controlling the lever on the keg doesn't mean you're better than the rest of us.

Don't be so stingy with the liquor this time, either. The last drink was so watered down it tasted like Lindsay Lohan pissed in a martini glass.

Cordially,

P.S. Here's your tip: you're an asshole.

Dear Asshole Bartender

Dear Asshole Drive-Thru Bank Teller,

I see you up there, judgmentally peering down at me from behind the safety of your bulletproof glass. Who do you think you are, making me push a button to speak to you and giving me dirty looks because I requested a pen? Get over yourself. Save the small talk and just send down the cryogenically sealed capsule, you snooty witch.

And out of curiosity, why must you always leave the window halfway through my transaction? I'm not sure where you disappear to for twenty minutes. I'm simply asking for small bills, not a three-hundred-page thesis on molecular cell growth.

From,

P.S. No, I don't want your smashed green lollipop. Do I look twelve?

Dear Asshole
Drive-Thru Bank Teller

GOTCHA AND **GOTCHA**
ATTORNEYS AT LAW

Dear Asshole Who Ticketed Me,

I was only one minute late getting back to my car, so how the hell is there already a parking ticket on the windshield? Inconceivable! Were you hiding in the bushes counting down the nanoseconds until the meter expired, you smug piece of shit? Where's my grace period?! I demand a recount!

I just wanted you to know, I'll be contesting this bogus ticket. I'll see you in court, that is, if you're not too busy trolling the neighborhood in your ugly little uniform ruining other people's lives. Thanks for nothing.

Screw you,

P.S. BURN IN HELL!

Dear Asshole Who Ticketed Me

Dear Greedy Asshole at the
Ice Cream Shop,

Are you serious with these prices? You're serving
frozen dairy and sugar, not scoops of fine Italian
truffles that were just flown in from northern
Umbria. I could have purchased a cow for the price of
that milkshake, and those sundaes better be topped
with a diamond-encrusted cherry with what you're
asking for them.

For all that money, you should at least up your
skimpy portion sizes. Aren't you embarrassed
handing those tiny cones over to your paying
customers? I've literally cracked walnuts bigger than
the so-called scoop you just gave me.

Lick me,

P.S. Freezer burn is not a flavor.

Dear Greedy Asshole at
the Ice Cream Shop

Dear Asshole Always Asking Me Hypothetical Questions,

I don't know if I'd rather fondle my grandmother or be eaten by a Tyrannosaurus rex. And I'm not sure if I'd choose to perform show tunes in the nude on national television or saw off my left pinky with a rusty butter knife. (Wait. Would I be able to use anesthesia?) The bigger question is, who the hell cares?

I've played along in the past, but I've grown sick and tired of your lame shenanigans. Sorry, but I have far more pressing things to think about than whether I'd eat your dead, frozen ass cheeks after a plane crash in the tundra.

Catch my drift?

P.S. I'll take the T. rex option, please.

Dear Asshole Always Asking Me
Hypothetical Questions

Dear Asshole Redneck,

Screw you and the muddy truck you rode in on! You're an ignorant, backwoods hillbilly and you wouldn't know class if it bit you on your coon-tail-covered mullet. Here's a thought: how 'bout you change out of your Dale Earnhardt pajamas and go see a dentist? In most parts of the country, having one tooth isn't a surefire way to attract a mate. It's a sign of periodontal disease, y'all.

Uh-oh. Your sister just came out of the house wearing a pair of Daisy Dukes, so you best run along and disappear back into your favorite camouflage-covered hole. I don't want you gettin' any funny ideas.

Yee-haw,

P.S. You might be a redneck if . . . you got this letter.

Dear Asshole Redneck

Dear Asshole Playing Guitar in Public,

It's lovely that you picked up a secondhand guitar book on eBay and taught yourself how to play a few chords. Hobbies are wonderful things. However, this isn't open mike night at a dive bar. It's a popular street corner. And no one wants to listen to you awkwardly strumming the same two Beatles songs over and over. You're driving me crazy! One can only hear the intro of "Yellow Submarine" so many times before you start wanting to drown yourself in one.

   Do us all a favor: pack up your little one-man band and go perform for someone who might appreciate your talents—like Marlee Matlin.

See ya around,

P.S. Oh, joy. Here comes the incoherent mumbling.

Dear Asshole Playing
Guitar in Public

Dear Asshole Taxi Driver,

I'm not entirely sure which saint you have dangling from your rearview mirror, but I hope they'll be able to help me survive this ride from hell. You're up there eating a pastrami sandwich and abruptly jerking the wheel, and I'm back here bouncing around like a ball on a roulette wheel. I don't have a death wish, so slow down, you asshole! This is real life, not a side quest in Grand Theft Auto. You don't earn points by running over pregnant women and fire hydrants.

If we make it out of this alive, tell Freddy Krueger I said hi. Judging by the slashes in these filthy backseats, he must be a frequent client.

Best,

P.S. There's an odor back here and I didn't do it.

Dear Asshole Taxi Driver

Dear Asshole with the Wind Chimes,

Take those annoying things down, you inconsiderate son of a bitch! They're driving me crazy, and I am sick and tired of suffering in the name of your tranquility. Besides, you must be brain damaged if you find peace and harmony while listening to large metal pipes slamming into each other at various octaves. It's not soothing or relaxing. It sounds like a four-year-old banging on a xylophone for the first time.

The worst part is THEY NEVER STOP. Day and night, all I hear is the excruciating jingle of those terrible torture devices. It's not cool. If I wanted to fall asleep to the ear-piercing sounds of amplified church chimes, I'd move to the Vatican.

Either you take them down or I will,

P.S. This is one situation that would definitely NOT be improved by more cowbell.

Dear Asshole with
the Wind Chimes

Dear Asshole Who Cut Me in Line,

I was under the assumption we all learned the fundamentals of line mechanics when we were in kindergarten. Here's how it works: first come, first served. I've been standing here for what feels like an eternity, and I'll be damned if I'm going to let a schmuck like you mosey in front of me like you own the place. It ain't happenin'. I put in my time, and cutsies aren't cool.

Oh, and don't try pulling that "I'm with them" maneuver, either. I can tell by your footwear you guys wouldn't hang in the same circles.

Buzz off,

P.S. Take one more step and you'll lose a limb.

Dear Asshole Who Cut Me in Line

Dear Asshole Who Forgot My Birthday,

I'm penning this letter whilst crying a sea of bitter tears, for your forgetfulness has bestowed upon me a sadness of unprecedented proportions. This is worse than the time the goldfish I won at the carnival died on the way home. Worse than the time my supermarket was out of cinnamon Dunk-a-Roos. And yes, worse than the time I watched that entire season of The Bachelor and that guy didn't even propose at the end. And I know you remember how much that pissed me off.

Now if you'll excuse me, I'm off to pick up the pieces of my shattered life. Oh, and I don't want your stupid "Happy Belated Birthday" e-card either, so don't even bother sending it.

Sadly,

P.S. Dinner Friday?

Dear Asshole Who
Forgot My Birthday

Dear Asshole Boss,

You're nothing but an incompetent, bullying imbecile on a power trip. The only thing you "manage" to do on a daily basis is piss off your employees and sneak out of the office for your two-hour lunch break. You just sit there in your little ergonomic chair playing Solitaire and buying things on Amazon while the rest of us do your work. Well, I've had it! Screw you and your Super Saver shipping, because I'm done doing your work and taking your abuse. You can shove your clipboard up your fat ass, because I quit.

Buh-bye,

P.S. I know you're sleeping with someone in accounting.

Dear Asshole Boss

Dear Asshole Smoker,

Shh. Do you hear that? No, not the sound of your lungs blackening, but the sound of me gagging on your cigarette smoke. Get that nasty cancer stick out of my face! Just because you enjoy smelling like the Marlboro Man's asscrack doesn't mean we all do.

No, I don't want to go outside with you while you smoke, so don't even ask. I have better things to do than engulf myself in a haze of your exhaled carcinogens while you pace around mumbling about your car payment. For Christ's sake, chew some gum or slap on a nicotine patch. I haven't seen someone so addicted to something since the time I taught my mom how to play Bejeweled.

Blow me,

P.S. You might want to get that cough checked out.

Dear Asshole Smoker

Dear Asshole Parent with the Screaming Child in Public,

Are you deaf? The ear-piercing shrieks emitting from your child's mouth can be heard from six miles away. We're in a small space and I can't take it anymore. Stop ignoring the situation and do something about it. Play peek-a-boo. Jiggle your keys. Slip them a Valium. Or better yet, just get them the hell out of here. Thanks to Junior's vocal gymnastics, I now have a headache and I can't even hear myself think.

Next time you're out in public with your demon spawn, be more considerate of the people around you. Because frankly, if I wanted to spend an hour listening to a series of high-pitched screams, I would have put on a Mariah Carey CD and saved myself the hassle.

Yours truly,

P.S. And the "worst parent of the year" award goes to . . . .

Dear Asshole Parent
with the Screaming
Child in Public

Dear Asshole Double-Dipper,

Ew. Did you really just slobber all over that stalk of celery and then plunge it back into the communal dip bowl? Wow. Way to gross us all out. Next time, why don't you just shove your whole hand into the bowl and forgo the veggie stick altogether?

You're not standing in your kitchen snacking over the sink. You're sharing food with other people, so show a little class. We came to this party to have fun, not to dip our edibles into a sea of your festering mouth bacteria, you asshole!

All my love,

P.S. Did you just quadruple-dip?
P.P.S. At least have the decency to rotate that shit!

Dear Asshole
Double-Dipper

Dear Asshole Who Stood Me Up,

I just wanted to say thanks so much for blowing me off the other day. I really enjoyed wasting a precious hour of my life waiting around for your sorry ass to show up.

News flash: this is the twenty-first century, you inconsiderate asshole! We all have phones in our pockets. You could have at least called to tell me you weren't coming, or do they not have cell service in Doucheland?

Here's to hoping you were at least off doing something important, like taking a class on etiquette.

Forever yours,

P.S. You're ugly, anyway.

Dear Asshole Who
Stood Me Up

Dear Asshole Clipping Your Nails at Work,

There's a time and a place for personal grooming, and a shared office space is not it. Not only is it totally gross, but I can't concentrate over the cringe-worthy clip clip sounds of your brittle fingernails being hacked off every two seconds.

We work in close quarters and there's a very high probability of a nail flyaway. Have you ever been hit in the face by a renegade piece of dirty fingernail? I have, and it is revolting! So leave the nail clippers and cuticle trimmers at home where they belong, you Neanderthal! Don't make me ask twice.

Most fondly,

P.S. If you come in tomorrow with a nose hair trimmer, I'm calling health services.

Dear Asshole Clipping
Your Nails at Work

Dear Asshole Who Left Dirty Dishes in the Sink,

The sink is starting to look and smell like a high school science fair project, and it's all your fault. This is a shared area, which means you need to clean up after yourself instead of just piling dirty dish on top of dirty dish like some ridiculous game of Jenga. Enough is enough! I'd like to be able to access clean running water without potentially contracting salmonella.

Oh, and a special thanks for leaving that steak knife submerged in that cup of stagnant, cloudy liquid. I almost lost a finger.

Regards,

P.S. It's been two weeks. Exactly how much longer does that pot need to "soak"?

Dear Asshole Who Left
Dirty Dishes in the Sink

Dear Asshole Picky Eater,

You've got to expand your culinary horizons, because you're driving everyone in your life crazy! It takes you fifteen minutes to order food at a restaurant, and even then you can't eat it without dissecting it like you're in tenth-grade biology class. Enough!

Your meal is fine, so quit wiggling around in your chair like you're about to eat a heaping bowl of maggots. There are plenty of edible things out there other than french fries and cheese pizza, so save the gagging and eye-rolling for times when they're really called for—like next season of Dancing with the Stars.

Best wishes,

P.S. Surprise! That wasn't chicken.

Dear Asshole Picky Eater

Dear Fanatically Religious Asshole at
My Door,

Turn around. Don't bother. Yes, I see you brought
a freakishly small child in a suit, but those tactics
won't work on me. I don't want your pamphlets
either, so don't even think about leaving one in my
storm door. There's only two people I open the
door for who I don't know, so unless you are
smuggling pizza or Kung-Pao chicken under that
scary trench coat, you best be moving along.
    And please, stop talking about "saving my soul."
Who are you, Jewel?

Warmest regards,

P.S. How long have you been walking around the
neighborhood like nomads? Haven't you people ever
heard of cars?

Dear Fanatically Religious
Asshole at My Door

Dear Asshole eBay Seller,

You lying, power-selling scumbag! I opted to buy it now because your auction description said the item was "barely used" and "like new." On what planet would that be, exactly? Because back here on earth, "mint condition" doesn't mean "smells like an ashtray and is covered in cat hair."

   I don't care about your stupid terms and conditions, either. I want a full refund! Give me my money back or I'll sic those heartless bastards at PayPal on your ass.

Forever and always,

P.S. Why did you charge me $12 shipping? It only cost you $2.50, you asshole!!!
P.P.S. I will not be leaving you A++++++++++++++++++++++++++++ feedback.

Dear Asshole eBay Seller

Dear Asshole Noisy Neighbor,

Awful music.. People screaming. Random animal noises. What the hell are you people doing over there? Running a circus? Enough! No one in the neighborhood signed up to live next door to the fucking Ringling Brothers, so quiet it down!

And lower your television. Are you deaf? Just once, I'd like to eat my dinner in peace without the sound of gunfire booming through my kitchen. At the very least, close your windows when you're arguing. I understand a flaccid penis can be traumatic to deal with, but that doesn't mean everyone in the world wants to hear about it.

Thanks a lot,

P.S. I heard you having sex. You're doing it wrong.

Dear Asshole
Noisy Neighbor

SUMMONS
The Court of Common Courtesy
Judge Hugh R. Screwed Presiding

Dear All-Around Asshole,

You're the biggest asshole on the face of the earth. If you were a Palestinian leader, you'd be Yasser Assholefat. If you were religious, you'd be an assholey roller. If you were New Age, you'd practice assholistic medicine. If you were in the Wild West, you'd keep your gun in an assholster. If you robbed banks with that gun, it'd be an assholdup. When you go out drinking, you always end up at an asshole-in-the-wall. You put asswhole milk in your coffee. For Halloween, you dress up as Sherlock and Assholmes. And if you golfed, you'd be the asshole-in-one.

Asshole la vista, baby,

P.S. You're the reason this book exists.

Dear All-Around Asshole